ICKY ANIMALS!
Small and Gross

WIGGLY WORMS

Celeste Bishop

PowerKiDS press™

New York

blished in 2016 by The Rosen Publishing Group, Inc.
⸍ East 21st Street, New York, NY 10010

First Edition

Editor: Sarah Machajewski
Book Design: Mickey Harmon

Photo Credits: Cover (worm) Maryna Pleshkun/Shutterstock.com; cover, pp. 1, 3–4, 7–8, 11–12, 15–16,19–20, 23–24 (splatters) GreenBelka/Shutterstock.com; p. 5 Joel Sartore/National Geographic/Getty Images; p. 6 (main) Ch'ien Lee/Minden Pictures/Getty Images; p. 6 (inset) Dimitris Poursanidis/NIS/Minden Pictures/Getty Images; p. 9 schankz/Shutterstock.com; p. 10 alexsvirid/Shutterstock.com; p. 13 TwilightArtPictures/Shutterstock.com; p. 14 (inset) Gregory S. Paulson/Cultura/Getty Images; p. 14 (main) PHOTO FUN/Shutterstock.com; p. 17 Kokhanchikov/Shutterstock.com; p. 18 Valerie Giles/Science Source/Getty Images; p. 21 John L. Absher/ Shutterstock.com; p. 22 D. Kucharski K. Kucharska/Shutterstock.com; p. 23 (all) andrea crisante/Shutterstock.com.

Library of Congress Cataloging-in-Publication Data

Bishop, Celeste, author.
 Wiggly worms / Celeste Bishop.
     pages cm. — (Icky animals! Small and gross)
 Includes index.
 ISBN 978-1-4994-0732-7 (pbk.)
 ISBN 978-1-4994-0734-1 (6 pack)
 ISBN 978-1-4994-0736-5 (library binding)
 1. Earthworms—Juvenile literature. I. Title.
 QL391.A6B565 2016
 592.64—dc23
                                  2014048531

Manufactured in the United States of America

CPSIA Compliance Information: Batch #WS15PK: For Further Information contact Rosen Publishing, New York, New York at 1-800-237-9932

CONTENTS

Have you ever seen a worm?
You may see them on the
sidewalk after it rains.

5

Worms are a kind of animal. There are many kinds of wiggly worms.

Most worms are only a few inches long. Some are longer than snakes!

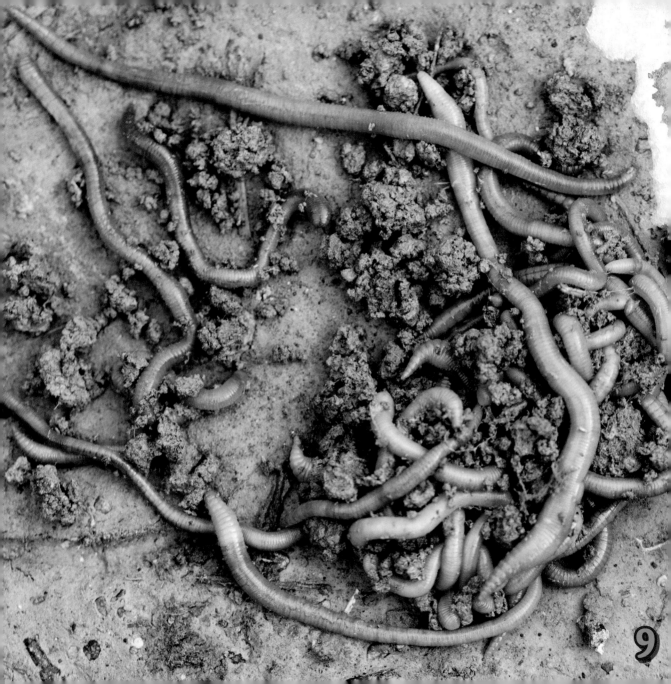

10

The most common worm is the earthworm. Its body is made of rings.

A worm's body is round and long. It doesn't have arms or legs.

13

worm-hairs

Worms move by crawling.
Tiny hairs on their body
help them move.

Worms live in the ground.
They dig through the **soil**,
which is also called burrowing.

Worms eat as they burrow. They eat dead leaves and **roots** from plants.

Birds love to eat worms.
Robins can sense where
earthworms are in the ground!

22

We need worms. They keep the soil healthy and full of air. This helps plants grow strong.

WORDS TO KNOW

roots

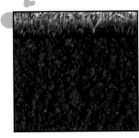
soil

INDEX

WEBSITES

Due to the changing nature of Internet links, PowerKids Press has developed an online list of websites related to the subject of this book. This site is updated regularly. Please use this link to access the list: www.powerkidslinks.com/icky/worm